elemental edition

fire within me

a *just write* journal

fire
within
me

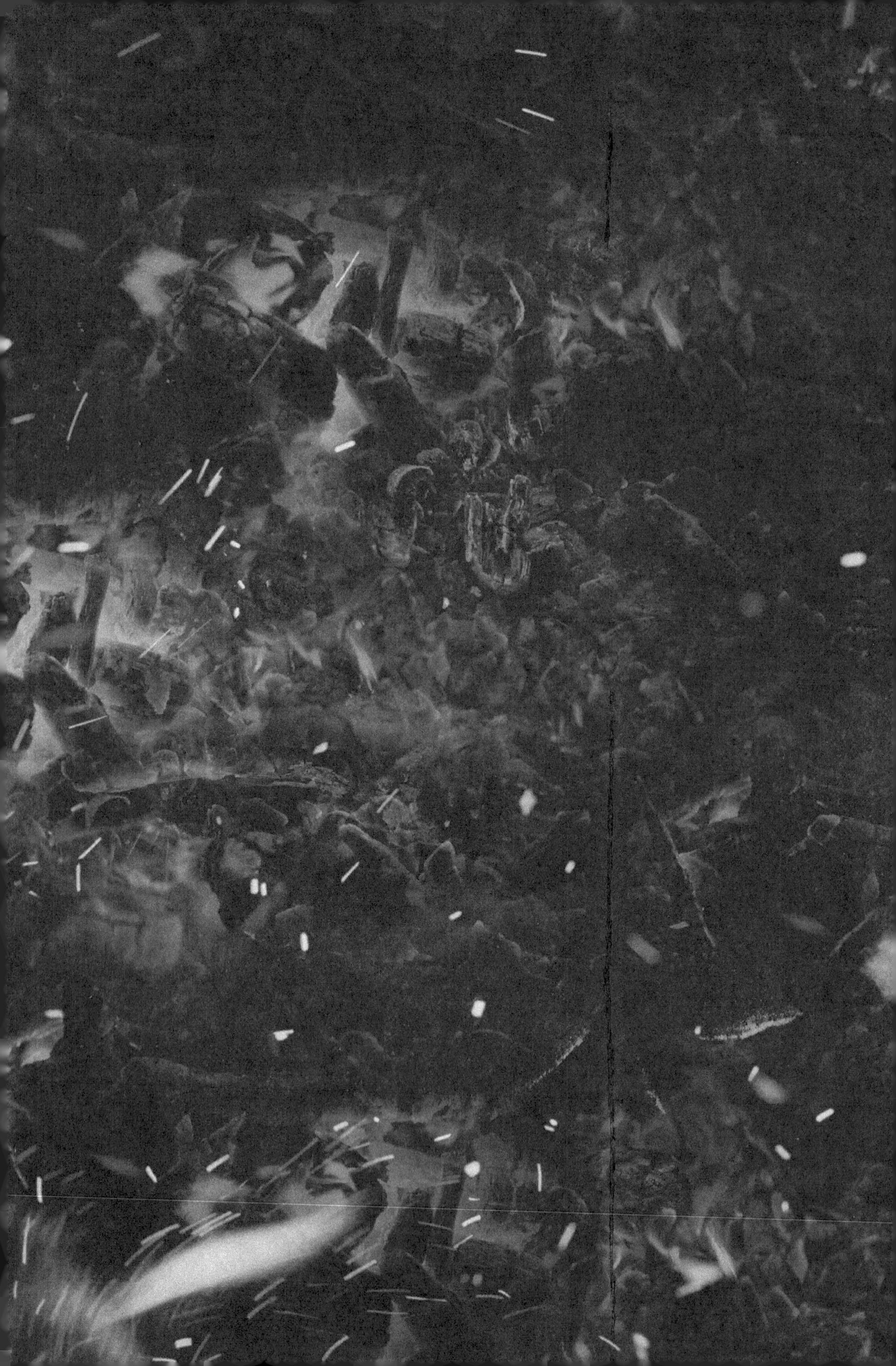

goals
&
deadlines

The fire burned and it felt like new beginnings. I could taste the ash in my throat when...

An extra hour occurs at midnight, when the sun blazes red and fire licks the dark sky.

I play with the flame between my fingertips. Some say it's dangerous, but I say...

free
writing

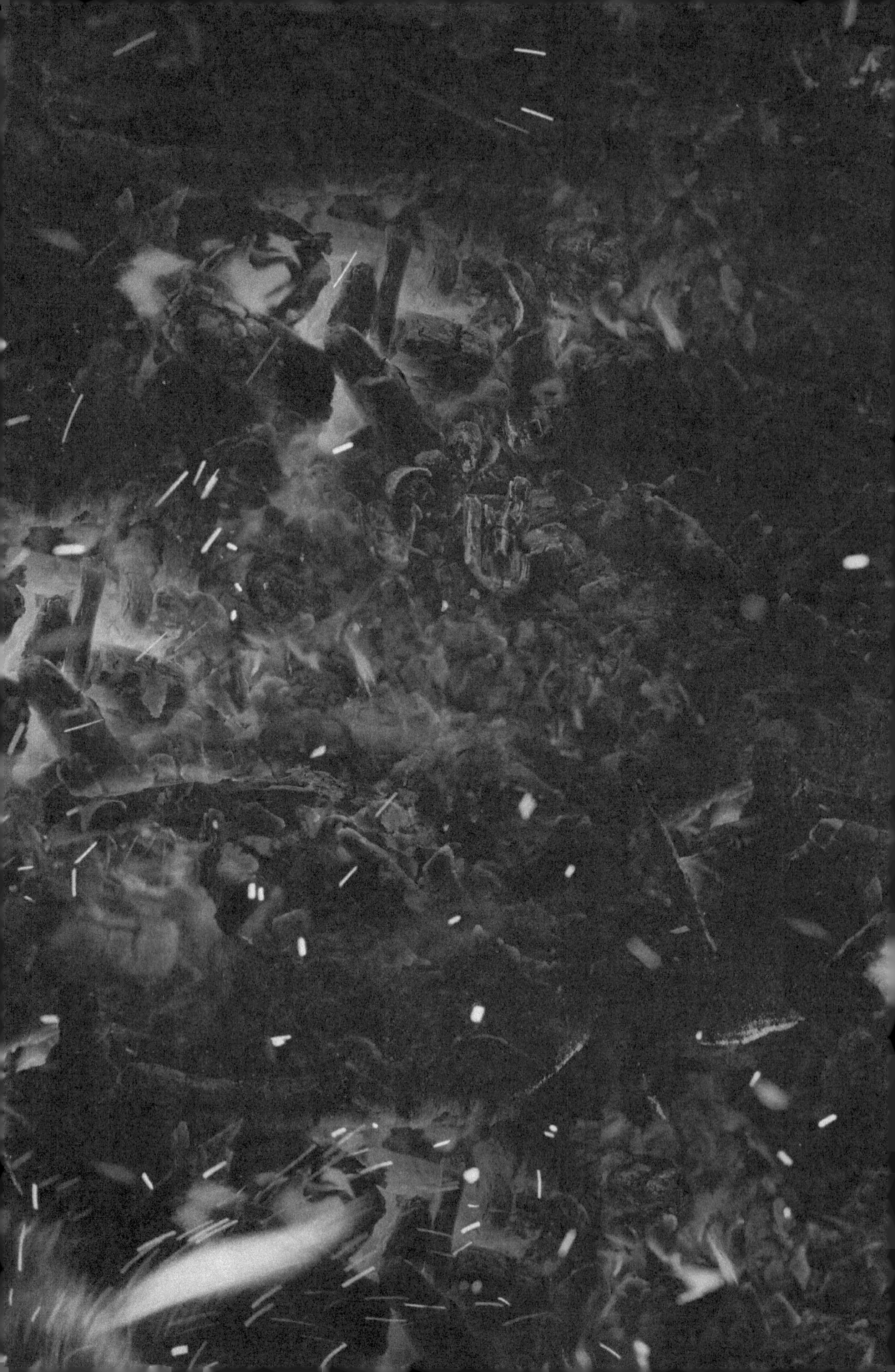

vision
board

write down your dreams
and aspirations, then
doodle/paste in images
that encapture them

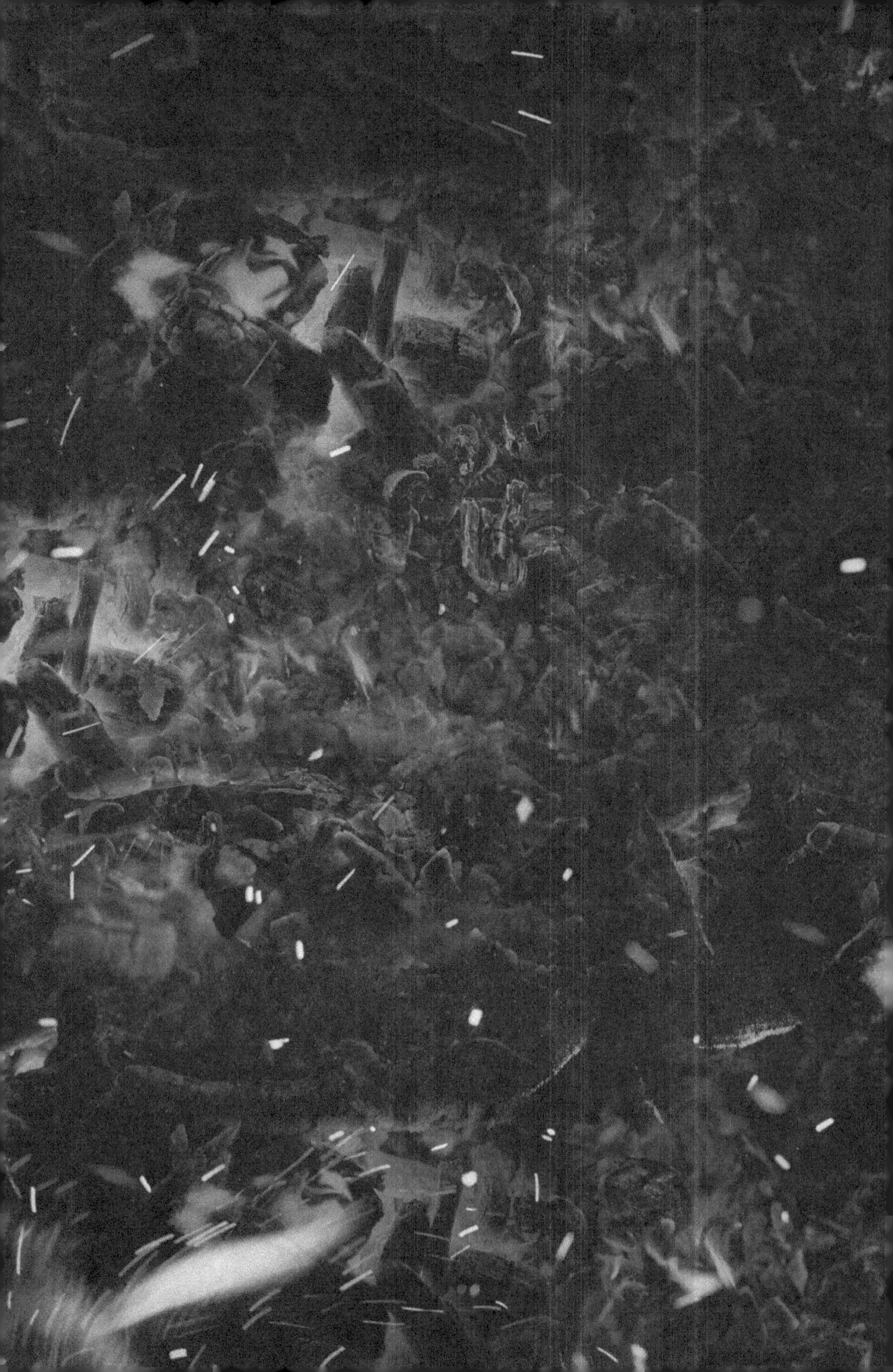

writing prompts

The flames rose high, causing a wall of intense heat to billow toward the crowd. The fire pushed us back with its force, and I couldn't breathe or move as I stared out in a frozen panic...

They felt alive, like they'd shattered every limit. The flames were theirs.

I watched in fascination as the sparks hit and the small wooden stick flared to life. I sat consumed by the one tiny flame wriggling wildly in its short existence. I tried to revel in the moment, because I knew after the match burnt out that...

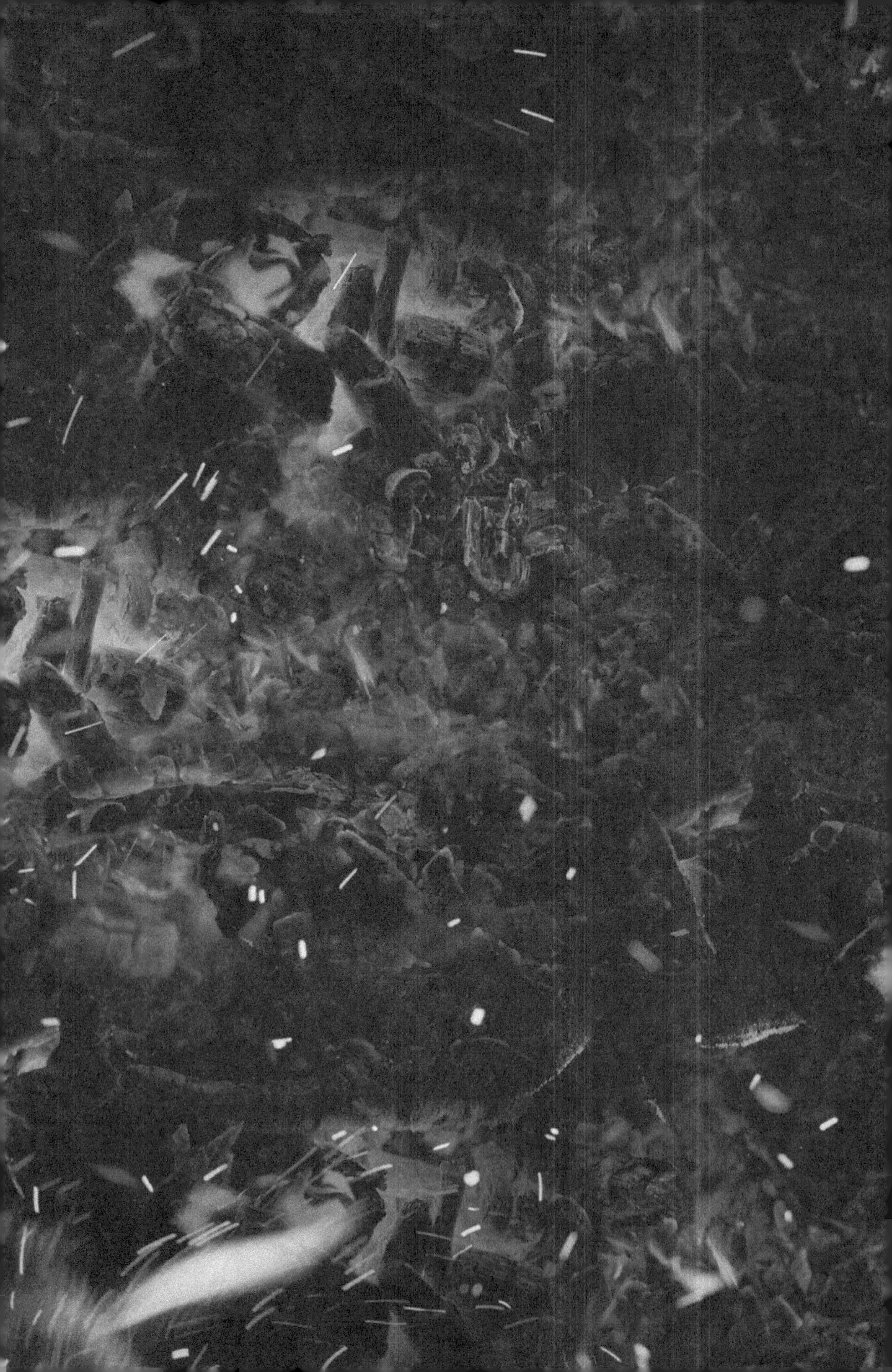

inspiring words

use these lists of words to
spark new story ideas

APHOTIC (adj)

Lightless; dark.

MONACHOPSIS (n)

The subtle but persistent feeling of being out of place.

PHLEGETHON (n)

A stream of fire or fiery light; a river of flames.

PICEOUS (adj)

Of, relating to, or resembling pitch; nearly black as pitch; inflammable; combustible.

RUBATOSIS (n)

The unsettling awareness of your own heartbeat.

DIVAGATE (v)

To wander or stray or to digress in speech.

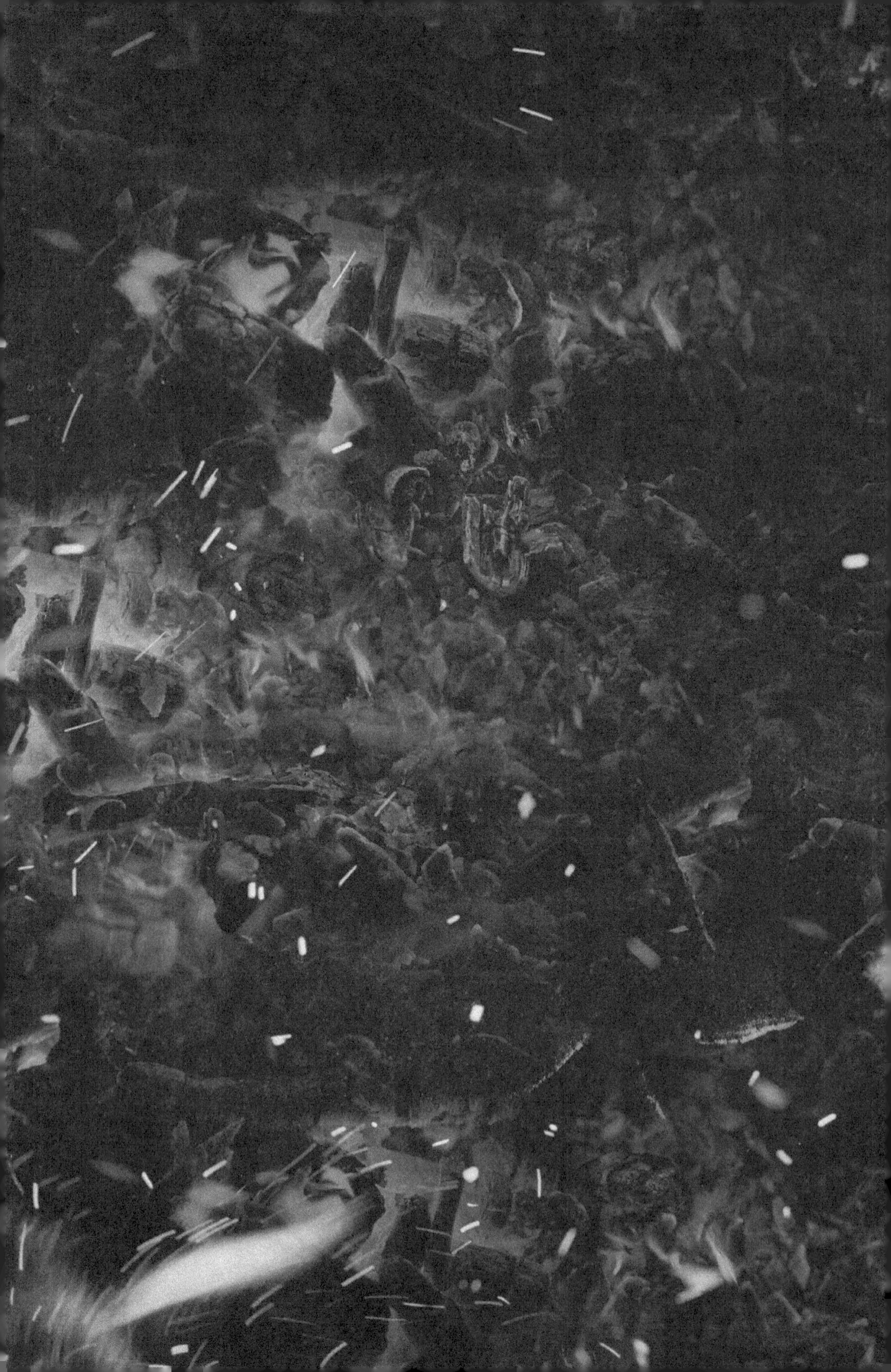

blank
space

about the designer

I graduated in 2006 from Brown College with a Degree in Visual Communications (Graphic Design). In 2010, I joined a forum and started doing fan art, using my design to make art from the books I read. While there, I met authors and the idea of covers and self-published work snowballed into what I've built today.